YouTube Takeover

YouTube Takeover

ALSO BY SPENCER COFFMAN

A Guide To Deception
Relax And Unwind
Work Less Live More
A Healthier You!
Affiliate Marketing Expert
More Facebook Everything
365 Days Of Devotion For Everyone

YouTube Takeover

YOUTUBE
TAKEOVER

How You Can Grow Your YouTube
Channel Into A Regular Income

BY
SPENCER COFFMAN

YOUTUBE TAKEOVER: HOW YOU CAN GROW YOUR
YOUTUBE CHANNEL INTO A REGULAR INCOME

First edition. August 2017.

ISBN: 978-1-9738284-5-7 (Paperback)
ISBN: 978-1-3709306-8-5 (Digital)
ISBN: 978-1-6622318-7-2 (Audio)

Written by Spencer Coffman.
SpencerCoffman.com

Discover How YOU Can Generate Income From YouTube Today!

This Guide Will Show You How To Start Earning Money Directly Through YouTube Videos, Without Any Previous Experience!

Everyone wants to earn an income without having to leave the home. Who wouldn't want to have the freedom to work when you want and to live a better lifestyle?

We've heard the stories of people earning **millions** of dollars on YouTube and we start to believe that they simply got lucky.

The reality is that thousands of people are generating a **full-time income** by making YouTube videos!

If one person can do it, another can do it.

We are all capable of earning a solid income online but many of us go about it in the wrong way.

YouTube Takeover

If you expect to have full-time results then you need to put in a full-time effort.

That means <u>treating YouTube as your business</u> rather than your hobby!

YouTube was designed so that even the least tech-savvy person can create his or her own videos. This is also true of making money with YouTube. Google has created the simplest monetization options, where with a couple clicks you can start generating money from the views your videos receive.

Any of us can generate money through YouTube.

But as we all know, simple doesn't mean easy.

That's why you see so many small channels abandoned even though some of their videos have a couple thousand views.

They couldn't transform those pennies into pounds. So how can you?

You Need Guidance

You can learn from my experiences and make your journey easier!

I've put together a guide to share my tips to help you create your own income streams from YouTube.

Introducing:

YouTube Takeover

You'll Learn:

- Why YouTube is the place to be

- What you need to get started

- What is takes to become a full-time YouTuber

- How to improve the quality of your videos

- How to get your videos found

- Building a community

- The importance of networking

- Generating MORE income from your views

- And much, much more!

This guide will help you to <u>start growing your YouTube channel</u> into a true authority, and will share some great ways in which you can monetize your views.

It's Time To Decide Whether Or Not This Is For You

With the popularity of YouTube a guide like this could easily fetch $30 or more! However, today you can own this great book for a very special price.

This is a truly incredible value, especially considering the significant difference it'll make in your success.

I want to share it with you and everyone else.

You will have the comprehensive and valuable insight that you need to finally become a successful YouTuber.

I know you'll be very happy with the results.

"Yes! I really want to discover how to grow my YouTube channel so that I can **start making money online** and turn it into a reliable income.

So please send me my copy of "YouTube Takeover" - so I can start getting more YouTube fans and finally making bigger profits, starting today!

Claim Your Copy Today!

YouTube Takeover

YouTube Takeover

YouTube Takeover

Table of Contents

Chapter 4 – SEO For YouTube
Thumbnail Images
Keywords
Title and Description
Channel Details

Chapter 5 – Sharing and Linking
Social Media
Websites
Viral Content

Chapter 6 – Networking
YouTube
Social Media
Bloggers
Making Friends

Chapter 7 – Generating Income
Advertising Revenue
Selling Your Products
Affiliate Sales

Table of Contents

Paid Content

Conclusion – Wrapping Up

Appendix: Resources

YouTube Takeover

Introduction

Let's face it. Everyone living in the world of technology has heard of YouTube. YouTube needs no introduction. It is an amazing video sharing platform that Google acquired for 1.6 billion dollars. Why did they pay so much for a video-sharing site that wasn't even that popular? It was because they saw the potential. Google knew that YouTube would become the most popular place for videos and potentially the second largest search engine in the world. Therefore, they bought it. They turned the competition into their greatest asset and now YouTube and Google are the most used search engines in the world.

Even though Google recognized the value of YouTube, it is still one of the most underrated platforms for reaching a massive audience. Businesses vastly underestimate the potential that YouTube has to bring more fans and followers. This is a shocking fact because YouTube has become increasingly popular. In fact, many people don't realize exactly how massive YouTube really is.

YouTube has billions of users and roughly half of the people online have signed up for an account. Since

YouTube Takeover

YouTube and Google are cohesive, everyone with a Gmail account also has a YouTube account. Every single day, roughly five billion videos are watched on YouTube totaling millions of hours of content. In a month, over 3.5 billion hours of content is watched on YouTube.

Every minute roughly 300 hours of videos are uploaded to YouTube. EVERY MINUTE!!!! Imagine how many are uploaded in a month! Let's do some math. 300 hours of video is uploaded every minute. There are 1,440 minutes in a day. That means that each day 432,000 hours of videos are uploaded to YouTube. In a month, that number is almost 13 million hours of content!

Through mobile alone, that means people streaming videos only on their phones, YouTube manages to reach more people between the ages of 18 and 49 than any cable TV network in the United States. In addition, 8 out of 10 people in that same age group watch videos on YouTube at least once each day.

Clearly, YouTube is something you cannot ignore. Google was right. YouTube had the potential to become the second largest search engine in the world and now it is. This is huge because it means that you can get as much traffic from YouTube as you can from Google. However, because YouTube is all about videos, the traffic you receive is going to be highly targeted and they will be significantly more likely to convert into customers.

Videos give you the option to really engage your viewers in a much more powerful way than regular written text. Videos are great for marketing because it quickly captures the attention of the viewer. In addition, videos can make a point several times faster than an article. You can literally *show* people what you are talking about. You can make them feel and inspire them to think and act. Answer these questions to help illustrate this point.

Have you ever been talking with someone but not really listening because you were too busy staring at the screen behind him or her?

How about staying up late watching something on TV that you didn't really like?

Has a commercial ever made you laugh or cry?

Chances are that you have said, "yes" to every one of these questions. These are all great examples of the level of impact that video has compared to written content. After all, when was the last time you were reading an article from afar while talking to your friend? Probably never.

YouTube provides this level of captivity and gives you access to the billions of people that are engaged in watching the content. You literally have a captive audience. You have an audience that is searching for one purpose, and that is to watch videos.

Another aspect that is so hugely important for you is the fact that YouTube comes with built-in social media sharing. This means that people can watch your video and instantly like, subscribe, and share it to all of their friends!

Therefore, forget paying the piper to create TV commercials on a network that can't even reach the majority of people. Instead, create videos to post on your own channel that people can search for, watch, and share with their friends all for FREE!

YouTube videos can have a lasting impact on your audience. People are naturally impressed with high-quality video content because it is something that average people cannot do themselves. Ultimately, anyone can make a website, add content to Facebook, and upload videos to YouTube. But not everybody can create stunning business and marketing videos that look professional, have high definition footage, great music, and excellent wording.

Therefore, the question becomes: Why aren't more businesses using YouTube? Clearly, it is an amazing way to gain access to a huge audience that is actively searching for the very content you are going to create! Come on, if there were literally billions of people searching for your product in a certain area of the world are you telling me that you wouldn't make an effort to put your product out there for them to find? For FREE!

If so, then your business is missing out. You need to take advantage of this free method of distribution, especially because many other businesses aren't. That means you have the potential to get ahead of your competition and be found a lot faster. You see the advantages. So why aren't people using YouTube?

Introduction

The main reason many businesses, perhaps yourself included, don't use YouTube is because they simply don't know enough about it. YouTube is so vast that people can't comprehend what is going on. Take another look at all of those numbers because in a few days they will probably be different. It is growing so rapidly that it boggles the mind and you may feel overwhelmed like you can't keep up or get a handle on what is going on.

You may have also believed that creating a high-quality video is difficult and expensive. This is not the case. You *can* create good videos. It will only take some time and effort. The hard part isn't creating the videos. It is knowing how to get people to watch your videos so that they can start bringing you an income. You saw the stats. Over 300 hours uploaded every minute. Your video will be like a needle in a stack of needles. How on earth are you going to make it stand out so that people will see it?

Fortunately, you don't need an answer for that right now because this book is going to show you exactly how to get your video out there. You'll learn how to get seen by millions of people through YouTube and also how to turn those people into fans or customers for your business. You'll see exactly how easy it is to start up your own YouTube channel and how to grow it into a reliable income. In addition, you'll see how you can do it without spending tons of money on expensive equipment, software, or anything else.

You made a great choice when you chose to read this.

YouTube Takeover

You recognized the value that YouTube can bring to your business. And after reading this introduction you realize now, more than ever, that it is time for you to become active on YouTube. It is time for a YouTube Takeover!

Chapter 1:

The Right Equipment

When you start making YouTube videos you need to make sure you have everything you need. Having the right equipment can mean the difference between success and failure. If you have equipment that is easy to use and that you enjoy using then it is a lot easier for you to do your job. In addition, if everything is set up properly and you have an efficient system then you are significantly less likely to become frustrated and give up. Therefore, take the time to plan things out before you start.

Professional Quality Videos

You need to create high-quality videos. It isn't enough

to simply film something on your phone in poor lighting with no script simply making it up as you go along. If you do this, your videos will look low quality. Then, by the time you work hard enough to get them seen, people may not even want to watch them. Therefore, you need to create high quality professionally done videos.

This isn't necessarily easy but it isn't hard either. All it takes is a little bit of preparation. You will need to prepare a script so that you know what is going to be said in the video. You may even need to have a rehearsal so that you get it right. Believe me, the less editing you have to do later the better. You want to have the video be as close to perfect as possible because editing is more of a pain than you know.

Therefore, be diligent and prepare yourself for the video shoot. Make sure you know exactly what is going on because you don't want to have to re-do it. Set up the lighting, make sure the camera angles are good, know the script, et cetera. You don't have to be Steven Spielberg and you don't even need expensive equipment. You only need to be prepared and know what you are doing.

Here are dome great tips that will help you make the best quality videos without breaking the bank.

Cameras
The quality of your footage is one of the most important factors in your video production process. It will define how professional your videos look and will be the determining factor whether or not people get

hooked into watching your video. If your quality sucks then people won't even stay tuned long enough for your content to pique their interest. They will bounce right over to the next video. It doesn't matter how good your content is, if you have poor quality then no one will continue watching.

The surprising part about this is that making sure your videos are high quality won't cost you a lot of money. In fact, it may not even cost you any money at all! As long as your videos are 1080p then you are good to go. You see, when you upload a video to YouTube the video is compressed. Therefore, the quality will go down a little. So if you record your videos in 1080p, when you upload them, they will be in high definition. This will also help your YouTube search rank, by the way.

Today, most cameras that have video recording capabilities can record in 1080p. In fact, most smartphone cameras are capable of recording high definition footage. In that case, you may not even need to purchase a camera! If your phone can record in high definition then you need to make sure that, when you record, you treat it as if it were a camera. That means it cannot look like you recorded your video on your phone. No shaky camera work, no muffled noises of moving around, and absolutely no rotating between portrait and landscape.

When recording on your phone you will want to keep your phone in the landscape, or sideways, position. That way when the video is displayed on a large screen it will take up the whole screen rather than only a strip up and down the middle. In addition, you definitely want to make sure you have a microphone. Otherwise, your sound will go up and down depending on your distance from the phone. Not only that but if your phone has the added bonus of recording in 60fps then you are in luck because that is something of which you should definitely take advantage.

The main limitations of any camera are the ability to autofocus on the subject and the quality of the sound recording. The autofocusing ability may mean you need to fix the camera on a tripod, or something, and then stay in one place when you are being recorded. The sound issue may mean that you need to invest in a little lapel microphone. This would be a good idea anyway because lapel mics are very cheap and allow you to record audio at a much closer range. This means it will be much higher quality, which means it will be easier for people to watch and understand.

Microphones
Audio quality is something that many people often overlook when producing videos. However, it is one of the most important factors when making an impression on your viewers. In fact, it is the second most important aspect of creating your video. First, of course, is having high-quality imagery. Making sure you have good audio can be rather difficult because, unlike video, you can't monitor the status when you are in production. That means if your audio is bad you have no choice but to re-do the production. That or record a voiceover, which will never sound the same when you piece it in and is often more trouble than it is worth.

The Right Equipment

Therefore, make sure that your audio quality is good because you don't want to have to go back and re-do your work. The good thing is that having good audio quality is pretty simple. You can do some practice shoots with your camera to determine the quality of the built-in microphone or you can simply purchase some microphones to use when you record. Due to the fact that microphones are pretty cheap, purchasing a few of them is a good idea.

The type of microphones you get will depend on what type of videos you are going to produce. If you are going to be recording someone talking then a lapel mic is the way to go. Even if you are going to be recording a few people talking go ahead and use lapel mics. If, however, you are going to be recording a scene of people then you will want to use a directional microphone. Something like a shotgun or hammer and anvil microphone will probably suit your needs. This will help filter out all of the background noise so that the important audio will be captured.

The bottom line is that you will want to use microphones of some kind. Go ahead and do a little research on what types of microphones will work best with they type of videos you are going to produce. No matter what, you are probably going to end up getting some lapel mics due to their versatility and ease of use.

Set and Background

Another important aspect of the video production process is where you are going to be recording. If you are recording in a busy area with a lot going on around you then this can be very distracting to your viewers. It can also make your video difficult to hear even with microphones. Not to mention, the whole atmosphere can distract away from the subject of the video.

On the other hand, if you record your videos in your bedroom then they aren't really going to look very professional. Unless the bedroom is the set you are going for that is. The point is, that you need to make sure wherever you are recording your videos is a happy medium between real life and a home studio. You need to be more than the garage band and less than a symphony orchestra. Find the place in between and you will be all set. Literally.

Try to find somewhere without a lot of extra noise that fits your video topic. In addition, you may choose to use a green screen background so that you can edit in a scene depending on your video. This could be a great option because then you don't have to go anywhere to stage your videos. All you have to do is find a good background and do a little bit of editing. However, a green screen is another purchase, and you have to have a large enough space to set it up.

Therefore, standing in front of a solid background like a painted wall or a tapestry can be a good option. It can be accomplished easily enough using a bed sheet and will still look professional. Make sure to shine a desk lamp on the sheet to remove any shadows and that the sheet is pulled taut. You may also choose to paint a wall a dark gray color. This will provide a nice neutral background that will do a good job of masking shadows. That way you can record at any time of day and not really have to worry too much about the sun shining through a window.

You may even wish to use a wall and hang some pictures on it showcasing your credentials or something related to your industry like comic books, posters, scenery, et cetera. The bottom line is that there are many great options for a background. You simply need to make sure that the background looks professional. That means it needs to be uncluttered, clean, and neat. If you want to take this a step further you can record using "macro mode" on your camera. This will let you focus on the foreground, you, while the background is somewhat blurred. Not only will this look very professional but it will also help hide anything in the background that may distract from your video.

Using this technique can also help you get away with recording outside at the beach, park, in front of a skyline, et cetera. All you need to make sure is that your choice of background fits with the tone and intention of your video. You don't want to be standing on the beach talking about how to grow a good garden. Your set and background need to go hand in hand with your video topic.

Lighting
Lighting is very important when making a video. If you have poor lighting then no one will be able to see what you are recording. In addition, watching something recorded in low light can be very frustrating to your viewers. You know the feeling. How often have

you been watching a movie and all of a sudden the characters go into a dark room or underground? You have to crane your eyes to try and see what the heck is going on. Don't do this to your viewers! They *will* stop watching. You didn't stop watching because you were invested in the TV program. They will stop because your video isn't going to be hours long and they don't have time to waste to find out whether or not your lighting will improve. Therefore, use good lighting.

When using lighting, you can do many things to add to your videos. You can use colored lighting that can make certain things stand out and hide other things. You can use spotlights, use lights to cause effects, change the mood, et cetera. You can pretty much do anything you want with lights. However, for now, all you need to do is make sure that your videos are well lit. People need to be able to see what is happening in your video. So, if you are recording in a dimly lit area, then get some lights!

It is important to make sure your entire face is well lit but be careful not to be in the spotlight. You are going for brightness rather than a beam of light hitting your face. That means you want an indirect light source. You want it to be bright, but not blinding. You can invest in professional lighting to help accomplish this, but it is much easier, and a lot cheaper, to simply take advantage of natural light.

Go ahead and record near a window with the light shining next to you. Having the light only hit one side of your face is a very popular technique called "Rembrandt" lighting. It is pretty appealing and looks nice. However, it is important to note that this isn't some "Phantom of The Opera" half of your face in the light sort of thing. It is about having more light on one side than the other but not enough to cause a lot of shadows. You are going for brightness, not some type of crazy effect. Therefore, keep it simple and make sure you are recording in a well-lit area so people can see what is happening in your video

Further, this should go without saying but it is worth mentioning. Make sure you look presentable. Make an effort to enhance your appearance and dress nicely. You need to look like you are on TV because you are on TV. Therefore, if you need to get some foundation to put on your face to cut the glare, then do it. Make sure your hair is done and everything is just so. You can't simply wake up, throw on some clothes, and start recording. No, you need to make an effort. You need to look professional.

Scripting
You can have the best quality footage in the world but if you don't know what you're saying then no one is going to watch it. This is why it is very important to have a script and know what you are going to say in the video. Then, if you mess up, you need to make sure to edit that part out. A little hint with messing up is that if you know you messed up, wait a few seconds before continuing what you were saying. That way it will be easier to cut out the unwanted segment.

Essentially, before you record anything, you need to have a script. Now, memorizing an entire video script is obviously out of the question. So is reading the entire thing off of a teleprompter. Doing so will make your videos appear like it is a robot talking and your eye contact will be terrible. You want your videos to appear as though you are talking off the cuff on the spur of the moment. However, you need to know what you are saying, which means memorizing lines. So, the question is how do you memorize your script and still make it seem like you didn't memorize a thing?

The answer is by recording short bits of your video at a time. This is a newer technique that is starting to catch on quickly in the YouTube world. What you are going to do is memorize a few lines so that you speak in short blocks. You are going to record a section and then stop. After that, you can take a look at your next set of lines. Once you have them down, you will record the next section and then stop. Then you will repeat this process throughout the entire video.

An important thing to do so that you make this technique look appealing to the viewer is to move a little bit with each new block of recording. That way you will appear to be in a different position. Maybe you move to the left or right, maybe you move a little closer or further away. The important thing is that you move a little. This will help blend your video together so that it doesn't look like a bunch of shots stuck together.

Doing this will allow you to memorize short passages of the script, recite them to the camera, move, and then repeat the process. You can then continue cutting from one clip to the next. This will give the video more energy and dynamism than if you simply sat in one place and recited the whole script all in one go.

When recording, try to be more outgoing and animated than usual. You can even be a little over the top and awkward. You need to act what you are saying rather than reciting or reading it. Many of your emotions will be lost in translation so it is important to be bigger and louder than you normally would be. The reason is that people know they are watching something on TV. That means they are unconsciously programmed to believe that it isn't real. Therefore, if you are being a little over the top then they will be more comfortable watching you, even if you are doing something in "real life".

The important thing to note when coming up with a script is to make sure it is detailed, to the point, and brief. People want to know exactly what you are going to tell them and they want step-by-step instructions. They basically want you to do it for them. Therefore, make sure your script is very easy for them to understand and follow. Add that along with your excellent presentation skills and they will be hooked in no time!

When filming, make sure to leave enough quiet space before and after each clip so that you can easily edit them together. At the same time though, keep your editing tight so that there are no awkward pauses or silences. That means you will end up cutting out much of that quiet space. Having it in your videos was simply a means of making your editing work easier.

Editing

Editing is the most painstaking part of the entire video production process. Therefore, when you go into editing, enter into it with the mindset that it is going to be miserable. That way, when you get done it won't seem as bad. Editing is the one place in your life where you need to make a mountain out of a molehill. Prepare yourself for the worst and when it arrives it won't be as bad as it seems.

When you edit your videos, estimate that the time it takes you to edit will be roughly six times longer than the video length. That means if you have a five-minute video it will take you at least half hour to edit it. In addition, make sure that you have your speech flow together nicely. Cut out those places where you said words like um, you know, uh, or any other filler word. Also, cut out any places where you cleared your throat, coughed, or there was any other unexpected noise.

This is why it is important to be aware of what is going on around you when you are recording. If you live near the airport and have airplane noise, maybe you pause when needed and edit it out later. If a dog starts barking the stop talking and start up again when finished. Let the camera roll. You can cut it out later. The thing to make sure of is that when something happens, you need to stop talking. Then, wait for a few seconds of silence before you start talking again. In addition, when you start talking, go ahead and repeat the last few words before you stopped. That way there will be a natural flow in your voice.

The Right Equipment

You want to make sure that your entire narrative sounds natural and has the appropriate pauses and tones. However, you need to be careful not to have any awkward silence that will distract from what you are saying. As with anything, practice makes perfect. Your first few videos will require significantly more editing that your videos later on. This is because you will get to know the process. You will learn to recognize when to stop and exactly how much space to leave around your throat clearing.

The thing to remember is that people don't want to watch something that looks like it was all scripted and done in a studio. They want something that looks and appears natural and spontaneous. However, they also don't want all of the mistakes that come with being natural and spontaneous. It's a double-edged sword. You need to use a script and edit out all of the human error, but you also need to appear like you didn't plan the whole thing out. This is where being over the top and acting can really help you out.

One final thing that is very important when editing is to make sure you leave at least five seconds of silence before and after your video. This is because you want to have room for branding. You need to place an intro and an outro on every video. Your intro, or video opener, is essentially a few second clip that goes at the beginning of each video. It will play a sound, show off your logo, and mark the start of your video. You may even decide to give a little summary of what the video is going to be about and then have your intro. Either way, you need to have a few second clip of your brand in the beginning.

Then at the end of the video, you need to have a ten second still image of your brand with a transition to it and a fade to black after it. You can also use this area to showcase other videos or promote anything you are selling. It is up to you whether or not you want to have any sound on this piece. Usually, it is simply an area to add the end screens on YouTube. Including an intro and outro on your videos is very important because it will help reinforce your brand to all of your viewers.

Other editing materials that can make a huge difference in your videos are the inclusion of music, using sound effects, bottom thirds, titles, and having your logo appear in the corner of your entire video. If you can master each of these, then your videos will look much more professionally done and you will make them much more memorable to your viewers.

Making Videos Off Camera

A small percentage of the people reading this will be thinking "No Way!" For some people, the thought of going in front of a camera is terrifying. Others may not want to appear before a camera for security reasons. Some people may simply be too lazy to go through the process of becoming "camera ready". Whatever the case, if you are someone who doesn't want to be in front of a camera that is okay. There is still a lot you can do in the video creation world.

There are many YouTubers who make a great living

by never stepping in front of a camera. There are still plenty of options for creating videos! You can record things like product reviews, tutorials, or how to videos with only your hands in the video. Or, if you don't want to be in the video at all you can record natural footage. You can record live events like storms, bonfires, concerts, et cetera. However, if recording isn't something you want to do then you can still make videos using your computer screen.

You can make slide shows or record video tutorials of yourself doing something on the computer. Many computers nowadays have the ability to record what is happening onscreen. Therefore, you can do anything you like on the computer while recording a narration. You can make tutorials demonstrating photo editing, software programs, coding, or how to do anything on the computer. In fact, many popular YouTube channels showcase people playing video games and beating tough levels.

The bottom line is that YouTube is a place for everyone. Whether you want to be in front of a camera or not, you can still make videos and succeed on YouTube. All you need to have is some knowledge and the desire to share that knowledge with other people. Then you need to dedicate a little time and effort into doing so and you will be well on your way.

YouTube Takeover

Chapter 2:

Logistics

Before you start your YouTube channel you need to make sure you are set up for doing so. This means you need to be in the right frame of mind and also have the proper equipment, space, and time to make your YouTube life as simple as possible. After all, the better set up you are the easier it will be and the more you will enjoy your work. Therefore, carefully read through the steps in this chapter because they are crucial to your success. Take the time and effort to make sure you have everything set up properly. You have to have a solid foundation before you can start building the walls.

Treat it Like a Business

The only way you can really start to make money on YouTube, and any other form of Internet marketing is if you treat it like a business. You have to treat YouTube like it is an extension of your business. It needs to be a part of the way you run your business or, if you prefer, a business in and of itself. This is the most important thing to understand about making money online. If you treat it like a business, it will begin to pay you like a business.

Many people think that they can simply sign up with YouTube, post a few videos that they made in haste, and then enjoy massive success and a lasting passive income.

That's not how it works. If it was, then everyone would be making money on YouTube, no one would be working, and the economy would crumble. Making money on YouTube takes work. It is a job. You must treat it like a job. It needs to become your business. I can't stress this enough. If you treat it like a hobby then it will pay you like a hobby. However, if you treat it like a business then it will begin to pay you like a business.

Many people make a full-time living from YouTube and live comfortable, and even wealthy, lifestyles. The thing you need to realize is that a full-time living means full-time work. They put in countless hours of time and effort and, over time, it paid off. Now they are living comfortably earning a recurring income on videos they may have posted years ago. These "Vloggers" or video bloggers enjoy a healthy income as a reward for all of their hard work. What's important to note is that if you listen to any of them talk about their business, they'll tell you that it is hard work and that they spend a lot of time on their videos.

Basically, if you are thinking that you can become a successful YouTube Vlogger who makes a lot of money by doing a little bit of work then this isn't for you. Making money online is not a "get rich quick scheme". It is something that you must work towards. People who make money doing anything online work very hard to do what they do. That means you'll have to work hard as well. It will be harder at first but the good thing is that it will become easier as you go along.

Therefore, if you want to make YouTube your full-time income then you need to treat it like a full-time job. You need to dedicate time, effort, and maybe even a little bit of money to make it work. You need to be patient and you need to learn. Don't worry; you will be successful as long as you are diligent, persistent, and patient.

The Power of Volume

There are a lot of little aspects that go into being successful on YouTube. One of these aspects is volume. You need to continually post content in sheer volume. It is simple logic. The more you have out there for people to see the better chance they have of seeing it. Now, this doesn't mean that you should start posting tons of random videos all willy-nilly. No. You need to be methodical. Your videos need to be well done and on topic. They all need to be related to whatever it is you are doing. They need to be in the same niche.

When you are first getting started, set a goal to post one video each week. That may seem unrealistic to you and a little daunting. However, it is achievable. In fact, it is a lot easier than you think. What you need to do is develop a strategy. You need a plan of attack. Fortunately, you are not on your own and you can follow this great plan for posting your videos.

The reason most people struggle to continue creating content each week is because they do exactly that. They create content each week. They are living video to video. You know, paycheck to paycheck. You need to be different. Instead of creating a video and then posting it. You are going to create several videos and then post them one at a time. You are always going to have five videos in the bank.

That means if it takes you three months to create five videos then you won't be posting any videos for three months. You need to take some time and prime the well. You need to lay the foundation for your YouTube business. Therefore, before you start posting anything, you must start making videos. Then, when you have six videos created. You can start posting one video each week.

Wait a minute! You say. Why six? It is because you

need to post a video and keep five videos in your video bank. The reason for this is because there is a thing that happens to us that causes delays in our plans. It is called life. There may be something that comes up and you may not be able to get a video done this week. Well, good thing you had an insurance policy of five videos in the bank. Next week you can make up for it and create an extra video to replenish your supply.

So, you are going to start creating videos. When you get six videos you are going to post one of them and continue creating videos. Then, you will continue to post one new video each week and continually have at least five videos in your bank. Eventually, when you get better at the video creating and editing process, you will set a new goal of posting two videos each week. However, that may be six months down the line for you. It is still important to keep it in mind because that is what you are striving for. Your goal is to post multiple times each week. But for now, focus on once a week so you don't become overwhelmed.

Let's take a look at the importance of posting regularly. You post your first video and it may only receive ten views that day. You may think that is a failure because there are so many videos on YouTube that get thousands of views. However, keep in mind that there are tons of videos that don't receive any views. Now, if you post another video next week and that one also gets ten views. That means 20 different people have potentially seen you. If you do this for ten weeks in a row then that is 100 people that have seen your business. 100 potential customers for you and if you are selling digital products then you might even make a sale!

Now imagine what will happen when you start posting twice a week. You will continue to receive new viewers and your customer base will grow. But more importantly, a good percentage of those viewers will probably subscribe to your channel. That means that your future videos will receive more and more views. Many of your existing viewers will continue to watch your new videos thereby boosting the view count on those videos.

Eventually, you will start to see your views and subscribers grow. Then, one day, one of those viewers will share one of your videos so that even more people can see it. In addition, your search engine optimization, or SEO, will be strangely better in one video and it will get boosted in the search results. One bit of luck like that could mean thousands of views for not only that video but for many of your other videos as well!

The cool thing is that it isn't really luck. It is something that you did all on your own by making your videos properly and posting them strategically. You also shared them on social media, which gave them an additional boost. Your persistence will be a great advantage. If you continue to regularly put out content then you are bound to get exposure. If that content is done well then you are even more likely to receive those highly desired views.

All of this becomes increasingly more effective if you are being as smart about sharing the videos as you are about posting the videos. You not only need to post your videos on YouTube, you also need to get them out there on social media. The reason is because many people use social media as their one stop shop. The "if it wasn't on Facebook then it didn't happen" mentality is truer than you think. Therefore, once you post your videos on YouTube. Use the sharing icons beneath the video and share your videos to all of your social media networks. Encourage others to do the same and pretty soon your views will climb and your exposure will greatly increase.

The more you do this, the more new fans you will accumulate and the more chance you will have at receiving a reliable income. Your goal is not only to get more views but also to continue getting views for years to come. And the more places you promote your video, the more people are likely to see it, and the more views you are likely to receive.

Once again, in short, it all comes down to the amount of work you are willing to put into your YouTube business. If you treat it like a job and you invest some time, a little money, and a lot of effort into it, then you have a much greater chance of seeing a large return on your investment.

One Final Tip

Doing all of this will mean treating YouTube like a business. This point cannot be stressed enough. If you're investing the time, resources, and effort you would with any other business then you will see results.

YouTube Takeover

Each time you post a video that is a result. Sure, it may not be getting thousands of views right away but it is still a result. You put your message out there for the entire world to see. It isn't going to happen overnight, but it is possible that the whole word could see your video. Unlikely, but possible.

Part of treating your YouTube projects as a business means you need to optimize. That means cutting back on your overhead and streamlining the video production process so that it is as efficient as possible. For instance, having a permanent spot set up in your home or office specifically for recording can save you a great deal of time. By not having to set up and tear down for each video you will be able to create more videos using all of the time you saved.

Over time you will develop habits, strategies, and tools to help you become more efficient and productive. You will become more knowledgeable and will be better able to create your videos so they require less editing. This will save you a lot of time and stress. Additionally, consider where you could place your script in case you need to read from it. However, make sure it is in a place that you can see without breaking eye contact with the camera or wherever you need to be looking.

In addition, you may also find little ways of creating your footage so that it is easier to understand where each clip goes when you edit the video. This can be especially important if you are having someone else edit your videos. Consider Hollywood and how they use the white and black clappers with the scene and take written on them. It is because it enables the editor to see where the clip goes and what they are working with when editing. They don't have to search through the footage to find out what comes next. This saves a tremendous amount of time because they can simply cut from the start of the scene they need.

Clappers may also help you sync the sound and video if they have been recorded separately. When you view the noise of the clapper in the editor there will be a sharp visual spike. You can simply line up the two spikes and you will know that the sound file and audio file are exactly where they should be. This is a strategy you may choose to adopt. In addition, you'll work out some tricks of your own to help yourself get set up more easily.

Things like placing an "X" on the floor or a tack on the wall can both help you know where you need to be so that you are in the camera frame if you are filming without a cameraman. In any case, there are numerous tricks that can help you when creating your videos. However, the best way is to simply get out there and start recording. Making good videos takes practice and it is something that can only be perfected by doing. You can read all the books in the world but if you never try any of the techniques then you will never get any good at making videos. Therefore, don't worry. Just start recording because done is better than perfect.

YouTube Takeover

Chapter 3:

Starting To Grow

Making videos was only the first step. Now you need to make your channel grow. You can do this in several ways. Obviously, the most important way is by continuing to regularly upload videos because without anything for your viewers to watch your channel will not grow. Therefore, keep uploading videos even if they aren't getting very many views. Then you can start to follow the techniques below to give your channel the help it needs so that it will be able to grow.

Building a Base

Once you are producing some high-quality videos and

you begin uploading them to YouTube regularly you need to work on building your subscriber base. If you thought getting used to the video production process was difficult, wait till you see what is in store. Building your base is something that hinges on the quality and professionalism of your videos. Therefore, once you have made some great videos, and are prepared to upload them each week, then you are ready to build your base.

There are a number of things that go into growing your subscriber base and many of them rely upon how you promote your videos. Therefore, make sure you take the time and effort to share your videos. Also, be sure to let your friends and relatives know that you have a YouTube channel. Ask them if they would be willing to subscribe and share your videos once in a while. This will be like pulling teeth because for some reason families don't like to fully support each other with online endeavors.

This is something that will likely change as future generations grow older because they live in an online world. Currently, the online world is something that the older generations don't understand. In general, people are afraid of what they don't understand and that is most likely the case with the current generations. They are afraid to get on there and support you because they don't know what they are doing or how it could possibly help. Don't let it get you down. Do everything you can to promote your business and if your family and friends leave you out in the wind then don't worry about it. You can still succeed. Chances are pretty good that they won't become paying customers anyway.

Make Your Videos 'Sticky'

You want people to land on your video and stay there. That means you need to have some great content that will keep your viewers interested. You want them to watch the entire video. You want them to stick to your video like glue. However, this concept goes even further than each of your videos. You want them to stick to your entire channel. Therefore, think of your channel as a Venus flytrap and each of your videos are like the lure. Your videos will entice viewers to see your channel and then BAM! The video will get them to subscribe and keep them coming back for more.

In order for you to do this, you need to employ some tricks to get your viewers to convert into long-term subscribers. Doing this is very easy and it can be done in each video. How you perform each of these actions is up to you, but it is probably best to do so in a variety of ways because some ways may appeal to some people and other ways to other people. Therefore, the more ways you perform these actions the more likely you are to broaden your subscriber base.

Subscribe
One of the simplest ways of gaining more subscribers is to ask people to become a subscriber. No kidding right? At some point during your video, go ahead and tell people to subscribe to your channel. You can do this at the beginning or end of your video. It should be a simple line telling them to subscribe for more

videos and stay up to date. You can vary the wording and placement in your video so that it doesn't appear you are placing it in every video exactly the same, like a cookie cutter approach. People will like the individuality.

In addition, you can also place some lower thirds or some YouTube end screens and cards that call people to subscribe to your channel. These are great text-based ways of getting more people to subscribe. As with the spoken request, it is good to mix it up among your videos. You don't want to bombard your viewers. However, you do want to be persistent. So don't be afraid to have a two or three different subscriber requests in your videos.

Like

Not only must you ask your viewers to subscribe to your videos, you should also ask them to like your videos. Liking isn't as important as subscribing but it is still something that you want to try and promote. The more likes a video has the higher it will be ranked on YouTube. Therefore, go ahead and start soliciting likes. When you ask for likes, keep it simple. Don't do it as frequently as you ask for subscribers. In fact, it is best to limit it to once or twice per video. Something along the lines of "if you like this video go ahead and say so" will be fine.

If you can get them to subscribe, that is the main thing. Chances are, they will like your video anyway if they subscribed as a result of that video. Still, some people like videos without subscribing to your channel so it is still a good idea to ask. This will help your videos gain more exposure because each time someone likes a video it is automatically added to a playlist on their YouTube account called "Liked Videos". Whether or not they allow other people to see that playlist is up to them. However, the playlist defaults to the public setting. That means that people will be able to see your video on their channel unless they have changed the setting on their playlist.

Comment
Not only are getting subscribers and likes important, but comments are another thing you should strive to receive. This can be done by simply asking people what they think of the video or if they have any suggestions or replies to what the video said. Often times, people will be more likely to leave a comment on your video than to like or subscribe to your video. Comments are a great way to engage viewers and help create discussion on your topic. This will help increase the exposure of your channel because it will seem like your video is "trending".

Share
The last, but not least, thing you want to get people to do is to share your videos. Sharing is very important because it puts your video out there for a mass amount of people to see. These people will see your video and be more likely to watch it because someone they know shared it. It was referred to them by word of mouth, which is the most powerful type of referral. What's even better is that these are people that you would never have been able to reach if your video wasn't shared with them. Therefore, prod your viewers to share your videos. It will do wonders for your channel.

You may feel bad or awkward about asking people to help you in this way but it is pretty standard for the industry. Therefore, make sure to do it. It will help your channel and you will benefit from it. As long as you aren't hounding your viewers then it won't be a big deal. In fact, many people won't even notice what you are doing. But that's okay, some of them will and some is better than none!

Often times, people will watch your videos and they may even really enjoy them. However, it won't occur to them to sign up for more. Then, later, they will try to find your video and won't be able to because they don't remember. Save them this trouble and remind them to sign up. Asking for subscribers, likes, comments, and shares is an excellent way to remind them to stay tuned to your channel.

In addition, don't be afraid to really explain exactly how important it is for you to receive these things. Tell people how much it will help you if they subscribe, like, comment, or share your video. You can point out that it took you a lot of time and effort to make these videos and that if they let you know what they think you would really appreciate it. It's a simple strategy but it plays on people's emotions so it works really well.

Shorter is Better

This is something that a lot of people don't understand. Shorter is better. If you make your videos short and to the point then people will be more likely to follow you. In addition, they will also be more likely to share your videos because they don't feel like they are inconveniencing their friends by having them watch it. You know this to be true in your life. How many times do you land on a page and immediately scroll down? Then, deciding that the page is way too long, you bounce off of it? It happens all the time!

The same is true with videos. If someone is looking for a tutorial on how to do something, they don't want to spend 15 minutes waiting for the 30-second instruction they need. They want to learn how and get the task done as quickly as possible. Therefore, make your videos short and to the point. That being said, it is fine if you have a longer video. After all, some things can't be explained in a short video. However, in general, try to keep your videos between five and seven minutes long.

If you keep your videos at a manageable length then your viewers will be more likely to watch the video all the way through. This is very important because it will help your YouTube rank. You will notice that there is a place in your statistics that tell you whether or not people watch your videos all the way to the end. That means it is important. The longer people are watching your videos the more status and promotion your channel will receive. In addition, if they watch your video all the way through then they are more likely to see your requests to subscribe, like, comment, and share. This will also help your channel grow. Therefore, once again, try to keep your videos short and to the point.

Create a Series

Another great way for you to get people to stay tuned to your channel and to continue watching your videos is to create a series of videos. There are several different ways that you can create a series of videos. You can either have them be "Part 1", "Part 2", et cetera or you can create related videos and have them appear in a playlist one after another in a step-by-step formation. Make sure that if you opt for the multiple part format that you label each video with "Part 1 of 3" or whatever your numbers are.

This will create a cliffhanger like feeling that will make your viewers more likely to stick around for the next video. Often times this will be enough to convince a viewer to subscribe even if he or she wouldn't have otherwise done so. As for the step-by-step type videos, you can place all of them in a playlist and then set them to be a series within the playlist settings. This way, when someone watches a video, YouTube will automatically queue up the next video for him or her to watch. This is a great way to keep people watching your videos and on your channel instead of letting them bounce all over YouTube.

Some channels consist more or less entirely of a single series. Some channels portray a story that builds with each video sort of like a TV season. In addition, some people make several short videos that are all one really long video. For instance, some tutorials or home improvement projects may take a long time to film.

Uploading several segments encourages people to stay tuned and ensures that they don't become bored or overwhelmed with a 30-minute video.

In addition, you can always break up some of your longer videos into a series. However, don't simply cut a video in half. Doing so looks bad and is more annoying than useful. A good way to break up videos would be if you have a series of interviews all on the same topic. Perhaps the whole selection of interviews could be put together to form one long movie. However, on YouTube, this would make a great series.

Of course, your video content may not naturally lend itself to a series format. However, there are still ways that you can encourage people to continue viewing. Perhaps you talk about what's coming next or give viewers a "sneak peek" of your next video. Give them a teaser of your most exciting content and tell them why they should sign up. Show them something they won't want to miss.

As always, make sure you are being as consistent as possible with your content. This not only goes for your video quality and making sure that you are posting consistently. It also means that you need to stay on topic and within your niche. For instance, if someone watches your video about gardening and subscribes to your channel and your next video is about marketing then they will likely unsubscribe because your content is no longer relevant to the reason they subscribed to your channel.

Build a Community

Another great way you can encourage viewers to continue coming back to your content is to build a community around your videos. This means engaging with your viewers in the comments section. If they post a comment or question be sure to continue the conversation by posting a comment of your own. YouTube will notify the viewer that you replied to their comment, which will prompt them to return to your video. This is very important because it makes your viewers feel as if they know you. If someone asks a question and you take the time to answer and also thank him or her for the question, how likely do you think they will be to subscribe, like, or share when you ask?

Another benefit of having comments on your videos is that, since Google owns YouTube, all of the comments that are posted on YouTube are also posted on Google Plus, as long as the commenter has a Google Plus account. That means that your exposure is automatically increased every time someone comments on one of your videos. Your video is shared to a social network all on its own!

This is great because now your video is not only shared to a social media network of people, but all of those people see that their friend is engaged in that video. This means that they will be more likely to check it out and maybe even join the conversation. Therefore, make sure you stay on top of the comments on your channel. Doing so will help you more than you realize.

Chapter 4:

SEO For YouTube

The act of posting your videos and remaining engaged with them are the two first steps to driving traffic to your YouTube channel. Without videos, there would be nothing for people to watch and without your interaction, they wouldn't stick around and continue coming back. Therefore, after a few months, you should start to see your channel receive more and more views. Continue regularly putting out more and more content. In addition, stay active and engaged with your viewers. Beyond that, there are a few more things you can do to drive traffic to your channel.

Remember that YouTube is the second largest search engine in the world. That means that your videos are most likely going to be found through people searching for them either on a traditional search engine or directly on YouTube. That means that you need to make sure your videos come up higher in the search results than similar videos posted by other people. It is a competition and you need to win. You need to elevate your videos and make them stand out because even if you have the best video in the world but it doesn't come up in search results then no one will watch it.

Thumbnail Images

In order to get people to watch your videos, you need to make sure they have good Search Engine Optimization or SEO. In addition, you need to have a good thumbnail image that shows people exactly what the video is about. Remember, a picture is worth a thousand words and, in this case, a good picture will likely be the difference between receiving views and not receiving them. After all, if there are two videos and one has an interesting thumbnail while the other is a random image of a segment in the video, which one would you choose?

Despite the saying, people do indeed judge a book by its cover. The same is true with YouTube videos. Therefore it is essential that you have a good thumbnail image. That means that you are probably going to have to create one yourself and upload a custom thumbnail instead of using the YouTube generated images. Don't worry; it isn't very difficult. Often times you can search Google for images to use and then put them together in Photoshop or another photo editing program.

It is also a good idea to place some words on your thumbnail so people can instantly see what the video is about. The key phrase here is "some words" not a lot of words. Try to keep the words to a minimum and make sure they are large enough to read. People like images because images represent so much more than words and they are a lot easier to see and remember especially in a thumbnail. Thumbnails are very small so, when creating yours, remember that less is more.

Another trick you can do to help people recognize your videos and further brand your channel is to add a banner on each of your thumbnails. This will really help when your videos appear off of YouTube, like on a search engine or on social media. Adding a banner is pretty simple and can be done in many photo-editing programs. In addition, they make your videos look very professional and significantly help to increase your brand recognition.

Keywords

YouTube works exactly like a search engine by allowing viewers to search for content and then showing them videos that match their search terms. That means your videos have to be tagged and keyworded to match the search terms. Now, this may mean that your video information may not sound like it flows or may not even make sense. But don't worry because it will make sense to the search engine.

YouTube Takeover

For example, if you want to know how to use Photoshop then you probably aren't going to type in a long sentence asking your question about Photoshop. Instead, you are most likely going to type in a sentence fragment or maybe even a couple of word phrases! The same is true for everyone else. People don't like to type because they are lazy. People want all the information instantly and they are not going to take the time to type out grammatically correct sentences when they are looking for something. You know this is true. After all, how many people do you know that use shorthand when sending text messages and emails?

That means you need to get up on the latest lingo and Internet abbreviations. You need to make sure your videos have the proper tags and keywords that people are going to be typing into the search bar. Don't be afraid to use the abbreviations. Remember, you are targeting 18 to 49 year-olds. Those are the people who are most often on YouTube. Therefore, they are your target audience and they are the exact people who type their queries in the search bar.

Therefore, if you have a video with great before and after images of a project or a photo you edited in Photoshop, instead of typing that entire thing out in the tag section. You will type as many variations of those words as you can think of. You may type things like "Gr8, B4, Grate," et cetera. The reason is because people don't worry about spelling when they search. They know that the search engine will automatically correct the spelling and suggest results based on what they meant. Therefore, when tagging your video, use search terms so that your video will come out on top, no matter how people search for it.

That being said, you don't want to tag your videos with hundreds of tags. Doing so will only harm you because it will make your video too broad. You need to hone in and be specific. Try to limit your videos to 20 tags or less. In addition, make sure they are all directly related to your video content. This will help YouTube suggest your video to other people who have viewed related videos, which will ultimately help your channel in a significant way.

Title and Description

In addition to having a great thumbnail image and several keywords, you also need to have a captivating title and a good description. Your title is going to help entice people to click on your video and watch it. It will work hand in hand with your thumbnail image to capture interest and spark curiosity. Therefore, make sure you have a captivating title that will tell viewers exactly what they are going to watch. People like to know what is coming next. They don't want to be surprised and they definitely don't want to be disappointed.

When writing your title try to write it in keyword segments. However, unlike in the tag section, you are going to spell things properly and make it look nice. Your title is something that needs to be appealing. Remember, people judge books by the cover so if the title looks bad then they are going to pass right on to the next one. The same is true with your video. People are going to decide based on your thumbnail and then your title whether or not they want to watch your video. Although on YouTube you will always have a thumbnail, in some search engines your thumbnail will not display. That means it is up to your title to draw them in. Therefore, make sure it is nice.

Your title and thumbnail must work together to draw people to your video. Therefore, write your title in two or three different search phrases that tell exactly what the video is about. It is a good idea to use dividers between the phrases so that people can easily read them without having to strain their eyes. Things like dashes – or vertical bars | will work nicely. In addition, try to place your brand at the end of your title so that people will know your videos even when the thumbnail isn't present. This is mostly for off YouTube promotion like when your title is hyperlinked on another site or on social media.

Channel Details

The final thing you need to do to help your SEO is to make sure you fill out all of your channel details. This includes making sure your channel name is relevant to the type of content you are posting. In addition, make sure to add your channel keywords and other details in the settings area. Fill out your profile and add any appropriate links to your channel page, including all of your social media links. In addition, select a good profile image and a cover image that depicts the nature of your channel.

It is also important for you to take the time to add some related channels in your sidebar and, if you are able, create a video trailer for your channel. In addition, try to create playlists and video selections for people to browse when on your channel. Place these lists and videos on your channel page by adding as many sections as you want below your cover image and trailer. You may have to switch from the default YouTube channel display settings to a custom display so that you will be able to edit this information as you please.

Another thing that many YouTube channels often overlook is the Google Plus profile. You'll notice that YouTube uses your Google Plus name for your YouTube channel name unless you specifically tell it not to do so. YouTube and Google are intertwined. That means whatever is on your Google Plus profile will work to help your YouTube channel and vice versa. Therefore, make sure you take the time to completely and accurately fill out your Google Plus profile even if you never use Google Plus.

YouTube Takeover

Chapter 5:

Sharing and Linking

If you want more people to watch your videos and subscribe to your channel then you need to share them. After all, if you keep them to yourself and don't share, then how can you expect other people to see them? You can't! Therefore, you must share your videos. That means you need to do everything you can to put your video links on as many different websites as possible. Get your videos out there for the world to see and encourage everyone you can to do the same. This will mainly be accomplished through social media sites. However, if you have a domain name you should also be embedding your videos on there as well.

Social Media

Social media is the newspaper of today's world. Many young people nowadays don't even receive the newspaper let alone know how to efficiently read one. Instead, they navigate technology with ease and fly around on social media sites gathering all the news they could ever want. With a few clicks, they have the ability to obtain more knowledge than a newspaper prints in a year. These are the people who are on YouTube. They are the people you are targeting. That means you need to get your videos on as many different social media platforms as possible. The more places they are, the more people will be able to see them, and the faster your channel can grow.

Try to view your social media pages as extensions of your YouTube channel. If necessary, you can create new social media accounts specifically for your YouTube channel. That way the account, pages, boards, or whatever will be solely dedicated to the video content you are promoting. In addition to sharing your content to the business specific social media sites, it would also be a good idea to share your videos to your personal social media accounts. That way both your business followers and your personal friends will see your videos. Not to mention, YouTube will count twice as many shares.

When you share your videos to social media try to use the sharing links within the "Share" tab beneath your YouTube video. By using these links you will tell YouTube that your video is being shared. They will see that the links under your video are being used and will assign more value to your video. If enough people use the share links, YouTube may even start promoting your video for you! Simply click on the icons one by one and post your video on as many social media sites as possible. Of course, you don't need to share your videos on all of those links. However, the more networks you reach the better chance your video has of being seen.

In any case, start sharing to social media from left to right. The reason for this is because typically, things are ranked in popularity from left to right. Since Google has pretty much all the information in the world, it knows which are the most popular social media sites. So if you share from left to right you will be sharing to the most popular sites first. Therefore, if you don't share to all of the sites, at least share to the first five. That will get you some pretty good exposure.

In addition to sharing your videos on your social media sites, you should also share some other relevant information once in a while. It would be a good idea to post some articles, resources, or affiliate products that are related to your niche. This will help keep your followers interested and engaged in your business. By sharing multiple different things on social media it will keep your followers from feeling like you are bombarding them with your videos. In addition, they may really like some of the other content you share and it will encourage interaction within your social media posts.

This is huge because the more interaction on your

posts the more value the site will attribute to your posts and profile. Eventually, the social media site may start to suggest your posts to people who have shown interest in related posts. That means that if you start getting enough popularity, the social media site will basically advertise for you and promote your content. This will do wonders for your YouTube channel because you will be reaching an audience that you would never have the potential to reach.

It is also very important that you post a link to all of your social media networks directly within your YouTube profile. This way, when people take a look at the "About You" section they will notice that you have social media accounts and will be more likely to follow you on those websites. In addition, on each of your social media accounts, place links to your YouTube channel and all of your other social media accounts. This will create an endless loop of links that will help to ensure that no matter where a viewer sees your profile they will have the option to click to all of your other social media profiles.

Another great way to maintain video interaction on your social media profiles is to continue posting videos even if you are posting videos that you have already posted. This is important because even though you may have already posted it, chances are pretty high that not all of your followers were on the site at that time. That means many people still haven't seen your post. Therefore, you can either repost your old post so that it moves up to the top of your feed and will then be seen again. Or you can simply go back to YouTube and share your video another time.

Sharing your video another time directly from the YouTube share tab is a better option because then YouTube will attribute another share to your video. This means the popularity will increase. In addition, when people see your post and navigate to YouTube, your social media standing will increase because the social media site will see that there is activity on your new posts.

When posting videos a second time it is important to post them on a different day and at a different time than you last posted the video. This is because some people may only check their social media on their lunch hour while others may check it in the evening. If you post at multiple times and on different days then you have a significantly higher chance of reaching your entire audience.

Websites

If you have your own website, then you definitely need to be posting your videos on there as well. YouTube makes this very simple by giving you an embed code to paste directly within your website page builder. In addition, if you would prefer to have your videos populate on your site automatically then there are a number of WordPress themes and plugins that you can use to accomplish this. I have done several reviews of such themes and plugins that you can watch on my YouTube channel.

In addition to posting your videos on your own website,

you should also try to get other people to embed your videos on their websites. This can be done by linking to them within the post on your website. Then you can contact them and tell them about your video, your website, and that you linked to them and would appreciate it if they shared your post. In addition, tell them that they should feel free to use the YouTube video in any of their website posts. Then, they may be inspired to share your website post on their social media page or even to use your video in one of their website posts. This will help you in multiple ways with the main two being as follows.

First, if they share your website on their social media then your site will rank up. Their followers will see that they shared your website and may go to your website because of the word of mouth referral. When people visit your site they will see your embedded YouTube video and most likely watch it. At this point, they are pretty invested in your content so they will probably navigate to YouTube to check out your channel and hopefully become your follower.

The second way this will help your channel is if bloggers start using your videos in their blog posts. They may write about something that is in a related niche to your video. Then, since they know about your video, they may embed it directly on their website. The reason they would do this is because it is much easier to use a video that has already been created than to create a video on their own. They will be especially likely to use your video if it is done well and really fits the topic about which they are writing. Now your video is on another website for all of their followers to see. That means your video has now been promoted to a vast audience that you would never have been able to reach on your own.

If you want to get your videos on other people's websites, then you need to start doing some research. Look up blogs that are related to your niche. Then, start contacting all of these bloggers and see if they would be willing to use your video in any of their posts. You may even explain to them that having videos on their site will help their website because people will stay on the page longer while they watch the video. In addition, you will be saving them time because they may not have the knowledge, means, or occasion to create the videos. By doing this, you can form several partnerships with bloggers and really increase your potential video audience. This will be discussed more in the Networking section.

Viral Content

You know what this means. Going viral is every online marketer's dream. This is the action by which your YouTube channel is put on the map. If your content goes viral then thousands, if not millions, of people, will see it. Your channel will skyrocket and so will your following on pretty much every social media site. You will have a guaranteed audience for all of your future videos and you will pretty much be set when it comes to income. Going viral is the once in a lifetime occurrence that makes your content an overnight sensation. Instead of taking years for you to start making a full-time income, it may only take weeks.

That being said, having your content go viral is not something you can count on.

However, if you want to really skyrocket your social media accounts and YouTube channel then you need to think about what will get shared a lot. Do some research on the trending topics and see what people are looking for. Find out the questions people are asking and see how you can answer them with your videos. This will be a lot of work but if you can create a video that satisfies the need of tons and tons of people then it is very possible that your video could go viral.

Even if your videos don't go viral, if you continually create content that satisfies people's needs then your channel will grow much more rapidly than if you create videos based on convenience. You will gain authority and recognition and people will be more likely to share your content and follow you on social media. Therefore, try to make the videos specifically for your viewers. This will make them feel like you care about them and they, in turn, will help you out as best they can. They will even be more likely to become a customer in the future.

Chapter 6:

Networking

Networking is something that is absolutely critical when it comes to your online success. Therefore, once you have established yourself on YouTube, you need to start building your network. Of course, it is never too early to start building a network. However, many people you will contact want to see what it is you are doing before teaming up with you. Thus, it is best to wait a few months before you start looking for any partnerships. In addition, when you are in your first few months you are still learning and getting the hang of how to efficiently conduct business. So save yourself the extra hassle and be patient.

Once you are established, there are many ways for you

to build your network. Mainly it involves contacting people who are in a related niche and asking them to work together. It can be something as simple as swapping links and sharing posts or even working on videos together. Basically, it all depends on how much you want to be involved with other people and how much those people are willing to be involved with you.

When contacting other people, try to look for people who are further along than you are. This way your videos will be exposed to a wider audience of people if you decide to work together. In addition, contact a few people who are beneath you. This will be good because they will be grateful that you are going to show them the ropes and help them along in their journey. Try to contact a mix of about 80/20. 80 percent of the people you contact should be further along than you are and 20 percent shouldn't be as far along.

YouTube

Try not to see the other people on YouTube as your competition. Instead, see them as your coworkers or, better yet, your teammates. You are all working together on the same platform with the same goal in mind. You all want subscribers and you all want to grow your channel. Therefore, help each other out. Make an effort to comment on some videos, add them to playlists, and like them. There is a good chance they will return the favor. In addition, if you develop a friendship with the owner of those videos then your channel will benefit because now all of his or her subscribers will start to see your videos.

The key to making this work is not to aim for the biggest YouTube channel you can find. Instead, try to find people who are close to your position. You can contact them in a variety of ways with the best being a message. You'll have to do a little digging to find a way to contact them, however, it will be worth it. Navigate to their channel and see if they have any social media links. Then you can contact them on social media. In addition, start posting some comments on their videos and let them know what you are doing.

Of course, not everyone will want to work with you. In fact, many people still see other video creators as competition. What they don't understand is that there are so many views that you really aren't competing with anyone. Take another look at the statistics on YouTube and you will see there are more than enough people looking for videos to watch. Therefore, if someone doesn't respond to you, or they don't want to work with you, then move on. There are thousands of other people you can contact.

If you are able to form a partnership then your channel will benefit in ways that you cannot imagine. If another YouTuber starts to like and comment on your videos because you guys have decided to work together, then that means he or she will help you promote your videos. As long as you are promoting their videos in return, there will be no reason to stop working together. That means that all of your videos now have the potential to be seen by all of their fans. What's more, is that if the two of your channels have similar content, then most of his or her fans are going to become your fans as well. This is almost a guarantee because you know they are already interested in your content!

Social Media

Networking on social media can be tricky. Since you already read a lot about how to use social media to your advantage when it comes to YouTube this section will be brief. Basically, in order for you to network on any social media site you need to stay on top of your followers. That means, that every time someone follows you, you need to send him or her a little message. Thank him or her for following you and suggest that they subscribe to your YouTube channel. In addition, you may wish to inform them of your other social media links so they can follow you there as well. This will greatly increase your following and will help your YouTube channel continue to grow.

Bloggers

Networking with other bloggers is a really great way to grow your entire business. Unfortunately, this is the most work and the hardest way to network. The reason is because you are contacting people with a shot in the dark. Then you are hoping that the message will get to the right person and that they will see it and respond to you. Many bloggers get hundreds of emails a day and they simply don't reply to them. Sure they may say they do on their website but, often times, they don't. Therefore, when you start contacting bloggers, do so with persistence and patience.

There are a few different methods to starting a network with bloggers. We already touched on one of the ways that is pretty effective. If you link to related blogs on your website and then contact them, they may share your post on their networks. However, you don't need to have a website in order to contact bloggers. No, all you need to have is something that they may want to use. That means, you can contact all the blogs you want and give them permission to use your videos in their posts. In fact, if you provide them with the embed code, they will be significantly more likely to use your video!

Therefore, start finding blog articles that are related to your videos. Then, start contacting those bloggers and give them both the link and the embed codes to your videos. This way they will be able to click on the link and watch your video to see if they are able to use it. Then, if they want to use it, you have already given them the embed code and they don't need to worry about grabbing it from YouTube. Generally, it is best to send a message about one video at a time. Otherwise you may overwhelm your audience and there is a good chance they may confuse the links and codes within your message. Then they won't be very likely to use your videos.

Another great way to get involved with bloggers is to start writing some articles for them. Many blogs accept guest posts and are very happy not to have to continually write all the content on their own.

Therefore, if you can write an article that is related to the topic of your video and then include the embed code within the article, that is a great way to get your videos onto other people's blogs. Not to mention, they will appreciate that your article has a video to go along with it!

Making Friends

As you can see, networking is all about making and developing friendships. The more friends you make the larger your audience will be and the faster your ability to grow. Therefore, make a huge effort to be as kind and courteous as possible. Be nice to people and help them out wherever you can. Then, simply ask them to help you out by sharing your content and following you on social media. Chances are they will be happy to return the favor!

It may also help you to think of all of your followers as friends. This may sound a little strange but it is pretty important. The reason is because you generally treat your friends better than you treat strangers. This way, if you think of all these strangers as your friends then you will be more likely to keep them around longer. In addition, if they feel like you care about them then they will be much more likely to help you out by remaining a loyal follower and sharing your content.

Eventually, people will start to look forward to when you post your content. This is especially true if you start posting articles or random updates on social media threads like Reddit. If you can get people to know your schedule and look forward to the day that your article is guest posted on a website, then that means you will really start to grow your channel. This is something that isn't going to happen right away, but it is something to strive for at some point in the future.

YouTube Takeover

Chapter 7:

Generating Income

Now that your YouTube channel and social media fan base is starting to grow, and you are connecting with people all around the web it is time to start making money! This is the part that you have been waiting for. In fact, it is probably the only thing you wanted to learn from reading this book. You want to make money on YouTube. Who doesn't? Everyone who puts videos on YouTube is hoping to be the next sensation and make crazy amounts of money so they will never have to work again. Unfortunately, as you now realize, there is a lot more that goes into this than people realize.

You mustn't be discouraged! There are several ways that you can make money on YouTube. In fact, there are so many different ways that you can make money online it is a wonder that more people don't try to do it. However, simply because there are many different ways doesn't mean it is easy work. No, you see how much work it is to start creating good videos and getting a following. The good news is, that making money is the easiest part of being successful on YouTube.

In order for you to start making more money sooner, you need to engage in as many of these methods as possible. In addition, if you come up with additional ways to make money, try to do those as well. Basically, you need to be hustling. You need to be doing everything you can to start making money because as your fan base increases so do your chances of making more money.

Advertising Revenue

Advertising on YouTube is by far the easiest way to make money. It is so simple that once you set yourself up for ads you don't have to do a thing. In fact, once you are set up, you can have your channel automatically set to monetize all of your future uploads. That way you can be sure that YouTube will place ads on your videos and pay you if people engage with those ads.

Getting set up is pretty simple. All you need to do is type AdSense into Google and register for an account. Then you can follow the steps from there and do what you need to do to make sure everything is set up properly. Then you will be able to link your AdSense account to your YouTube channel by becoming a YouTube Partner. This basically means that you are verified and able to have ads on your videos.

In general, you can expect to make about one dollar for every 1,000 views you get on YouTube. Therefore, you need to get lots and lots of views in order for you to make YouTube a full-time income. In addition, you need to have tons of subscribers so that you can continue getting those views. Generally, you can expect to start making real money when your subscriber count reaches 30,000 people. At that point you will probably be making an average income. You aren't going to be rich, but you won't be below the poverty line either.

Of course, the more people engage with your ads the more money you can make. Therefore, if you receive 1,000 views and 500 people click on your ads you are going to make a lot more than one dollar. The more people engage with your content the more value YouTube associates with it. In addition, the more views on each of your videos the more you get paid for each ad that will appear there. The reason is because YouTube recognizes that your video is getting traffic. That means the ads on your video are more likely to be seen if they are on your video than if they are on a video that receives less traffic. Therefore, they can charge more for ad placement on your video. When they charge more, you get paid more. It's as simple as that.

If you choose, YouTube will place a few different types of ads on your videos. They may show a full preview, banner ad, or popups. With YouTube ads there are two ways you can make money. The first way is if someone watches the ad on your video all the way through. That means they don't skip the ad and go straight to the video or they don't close the ad if it pops up when they are watching the video. The second way is if someone clicks on the ad in your video. Obviously, you will be paid more if someone clicks on the ad as opposed to if someone only watches the ad.

Now, one thing that you need to be smart about is not clicking on your own ads. You can't simply start telling all of your friends to watch your videos and click on your ads so you get paid more. No. Google monitors the clicks and they will know whether or not you were really interested in the content of that ad or if you were simply clicking on it to boost your income. In fact, if they detect that your ads are getting false clicks they may even ban you from the AdSense program. That would suck because then you wouldn't be able to make any money from Google AdSense on YouTube or on any of your websites.

Another cautionary statement is to wait to place ads on your videos until you are getting several hundred views on your videos and have at least 1000 subscribers. This is important because YouTube may revoke your partnership if they think your channel isn't generating enough traffic to justify charging their customers to place ads there. In addition, Google may suspend your AdSense account if they determine that your websites aren't receiving enough traffic.

Therefore, before placing ads on your YouTube videos,

or on your website, make sure you are continually getting enough engagement. For YouTube this means meeting the YouTube partner requirements. For your website it means having at least 500 hits a month. Even though you want to make money as soon as possible it is best to be patient and wait until you have the traffic. This way there will not be any problems down the road and you can continue to be paid for ads well into the future.

Selling Your Products

Another option of making money with your YouTube videos that you can do at any time is selling your own products. Since they are your products you don't have to worry about any regulations or restrictions when it comes to selling them on your YouTube channel. In addition, you can also place links to sell your products within your social media pages and in any guest posts you may write for bloggers.

When selling your products on YouTube it is important to note that people usually aren't watching your videos with the intention of making a purchase. Of course, if you are reviewing products then they may be thinking about purchasing something, and in that case, you can direct them to making that purchase. However, generally, they are not thinking about purchasing *your* product. Therefore, when promoting your products, do so lightly. Simply place a link or two in the description, add a notification card, and you can mention it in the video.

You can sell any kind of product exactly as you would in real life. Remember, that if you start promoting your products within your YouTube videos then you better never stop selling those products. If you do, then you'll have to take down the video and sabotage your view count. In addition, be prepared to field questions about the products and make sure you are set up for distribution. Whether your products are physical or digital you will most likely want to have a website so that people can browse all of your other products as well.

Placing products on your channel will help both your sales and your YouTube channel. This is because people who are loyal to your channel will begin to become loyal to your brand. That means, when they see that you are selling something, they will be more likely to trust that it is a quality product. In the same way, your customers who also trust you and like your products will see that you have a YouTube channel and will likely subscribe to it because they have purchased from you in the past. Therefore, it is a pretty good system that will work hand in hand to build both your customer base and your fan base.

Affiliate Sales

If you don't have your own products to sell then why not sell products for other people? In fact, even if you are selling your own products, you should still consider promoting other products as well. Being an affiliate salesman is very easy to do and won't cost you a thing. Basically, you are going to promote products for other people and they will pay you a commission on each sale. The commission you receive will vary depending on the product and the vendor. For instance, Amazon pays roughly three percent for most of their products. However, if you sell my eBooks, I'll give you 100 percent of the sale!

There are many websites for which you can become an affiliate marketer. Several of the most popular are Amazon, eBay, Click Bank, Commission Junction, and JVZoo. There are thousands and thousands more, but those will be enough to get you started. In fact, if you want to get started with as little hassle as possible, sign up for Amazon only. That is really the only one you need because virtually everyone online has an Amazon account and you can buy pretty much anything on their website. Therefore, no matter what you have in your video, there is a pretty good possibility it is on Amazon.

It is important to note that some networks like Commission Junction will suspend your account if you don't make enough sales each quarter. You can reopen your account, but still, it is somewhat of a hassle when you are first starting out. Therefore, before signing up for any affiliate program, consider what products you are going to promote. Then find out where those products are sold and sign up to become an affiliate for that retailer. In addition, it would be a very good idea for you to read Affiliate Marketing Expert to learn more about how you can make money affiliate marketing.

Affiliate marketing will be a great source of income

for you if you have videos that use any products. In addition, if you are reviewing products then it will be especially good for you to be an affiliate for them. All you need to do is place your affiliate link in the video description and then let people know that a link will be down in the description in case they wish to purchase the products.

It is important to note that you are probably not going to make significant amounts of money through affiliate commissions on YouTube. In fact, you will most likely make more money through ads than through affiliate links. However, that doesn't mean it isn't worth doing. As your channel grows, more and more people will see your videos and that means more people will be able to click on your affiliate links. Eventually, you will start seeing some sales. However, generally, people who make money doing affiliate marketing are doing so on their own websites and blogs.

Paid Content

Another way that you can use YouTube to start making money is by offering paid content. This means that rather than having your videos free for people to watch you will charge them to watch. Unless you are putting out some pretty amazing content, don't rely too heavily on this method of income. The reason is because there are thousands of other people on YouTube who have videos that are similar to yours and their videos are most likely free. Even if there aren't any free videos on YouTube there is a pretty good chance that Google will have something that is free.

Generating Income

Therefore, keep your videos free until you start generating a large fan base. Then, a great way to capitalize on paid content is to create a series of videos in which the latter videos in the series require a payment. This strategy will get people hooked on the series of videos then they will be more likely to make a payment because they have already invested the time in the series. Not to mention, they will most likely be interested enough to continue so paying a few bucks isn't going to stop them.

When selecting a price for your content, keep it low. Your goal is to have many people pay to watch it, not to have only one person pay to watch it. That means you need to make it cheap enough so that it is a no-brainer for someone to pay for. Basically, make it $0.99 or $1.99. If you really gain a large following then you can increase the price because you know that out of thousands of subscribers there will be enough people that will pay a premium for the content you are offering.

YouTube Takeover

Conclusion:

Wrapping Up

There you have it. That is pretty much everything you need to know to get started on YouTube and set yourself up to turn it into a steady reliable income. Of course, there is so much more to learn. However, much of that can only be learned by doing so the most important thing is to get started as soon as you can. Make a plan and get yourself set up so you can start cranking out the videos. Remember the steps and techniques discussed earlier because they are essential for your success.

As you start progressing along, you will discover that you are getting better and better at your job. It is like anything, practice makes perfect and you need a lot of practice. The only way you are going to get practice is if you make the decision to start doing it. It won't be long and you will start to notice dramatic improvements in your video production process.

Remember not to be discouraged because it can take some time to get a system going. In addition, try to make videos on a topic you enjoy. That way it will be a lot easier for you to go through the process. Especially when you are first learning how to do everything. Not only that, but when you are working on something you enjoy it is almost like you aren't working at all. You will simply be spending your time doing something you love. Then, later on, you'll get paid for it!

Here is a brief bullet-point list of the main topics we covered and that you need to work on when building your YouTube channel.

- Treat it like a business
- Creating high quality videos
- Regularly uploading your videos
- Taking a systematic approach
- Focusing on SEO
- Sharing to social media
- Coming up with interesting topics and titles
- Building a community
- Networking and forming partnerships
- Generating some income

If you work hard at achieving each of these tasks one at a time then it will be much easier than if you attempt to accomplish them all at once. In addition, you will find it much more rewarding if you can monitor your progress as you move forward. Therefore, take your time and don't expect everything to happen overnight. Remember, you are building a business and building a business takes time, hard work, and a lot of effort. Don't be discouraged because the payoff here is huge. If you stick with it and apply yourself it is very possible that you will be able to make a full-time living on YouTube.

YouTube Takeover

Appendix:

Resources

Spencer Coffman YouTube Channels
https://spencercoffman.com/youtube-channels

Sell My eBooks and Get 100%
https://www.jvzoo.com/sellers/user/544713

YouTube Takeover

About The Author

Spencer Coffman is proficient in many video editing programs and has created hundreds of videos. He has managed several successful YouTube channels and knows what it takes to make video production a job rather than a hobby. Now he is sharing that information with you. Go ahead and grab your copy today! To read more about Spencer, visit his website spencercoffman.com

YouTube Takeover

About The Author

YouTube Takeover

www.ingramcontent.com/pod-product-compliance
Lightning Source LLC
La Vergne TN
LVHW052306060326
832902LV00021B/3734